Kids Can Know the Way

Session	Theme	Kids Can Know the Way	Kids Create	Kids Move
Kickoff	Begin on the Way	Luke 2:39-52 We can learn about God, just like Jesus did.	Learn at the temple; Travel to the temple; Make an imprint	Pack for the journey relay; Travel to the temple; Where is Jesus?; Closer to God
1	Learn from the Teacher	Luke 4:14-30, 42-44 Jesus shows us how to proclaim the way.	News report; Take the Word; Plan a worship service	Five senses tour; Who is calling?; Release tag
2	Follow the Call	Luke 5:1-11 Mark 3:13-19 We can follow Jesus' call.	How we follow Jesus; Fish nets; We each do our part	Fish in the net; Sardines; Follow the call
3	Bear Good Fruit	Matthew 7:15-20 Luke 6:43-45 We can grow good fruit.	Fruit of the spirit tree; Kindness kabobs; Fruit search	Gather the fruit scavenger hunt; Act out the fruits; Fruit tasting
4	Help a Friend	Mark 2:3-12 Jesus calls us to help others.	Through the roof; Friends helping friends collage; Be an encourager	Move the friend; Work with a friend race; Help carry the load
5	Plant Seeds	Luke 8:4-15 Seeds grow in good soil.	Plant a seed in good ground; Bird feeders; Tending the soil of your heart	Act it out; Sower and seeds course; Save the seed; Weeding project
6	Share Gifts	Mark 6:30-44 Jesus will use our gifts.	Blessing bags; Bracelets to share; Sharing my gifts coupons	Mixed-up picnic; Work together; Multiplying loaves
7	Know the Shepherd	Luke 15:3-7 Matthew 18:12-14 Jesus is the Good Shepherd.	Decode a verse; Paint a path; Rejoice mural	Find the sheep; Sheep in a haystack; Hear the shepherd's voice; Listen to one another
8	Share the Way	Luke 10:38-42 We can welcome others.	Ways to welcome; Story strips; Plan a party	Make a visit; Hospitality cafe; Role play; Room for more
Closing	Friends Share the Way	Luke 8:1-3 Jesus' friends share the way.	Know the way mural; Act out the Bible stories; Share the story; Don't hit the trail hungry; Have you seen Jesus; Prayer pockets; Pass the message	

KIDS CAN KNOW THE WAY

The following titles were used in the writing of *Kids Can Know the Way:*
- Klippenstein, LaVerna. *The Savior Comes*. Grades 3 and 4, The Foundation Series. Newton, KS: Faith and Life Press, 1981.
- Kym, Betta. *Stories by the Sea*. Newton, KS: Faith and Life Press, 1991.
- Snyder, Eleanor, project director. *Jesus Friends*. Vacation Bible School. Scottdale, PA: Faith & Life Resources, 2005.

Copyright © 2013 by MennoMedia, Harrisonburg, Virginia 22802
  Released simultaneously in Canada by Faith & Life Resources,
  Waterloo, Ontario N2L 6H7. All rights reserved.
International Standard Book Number: 978-0-8361-9696-2
Printed in United States of America
Cover photo by Stockbyte/Stockbyte/Thinkstock
Cover design by Reuben Graham
Writer: Amy Nissley Stauffer, Project Director: Mary Ann Weber, Editor: Lauren Stoltzfus, Designer: Reuben Graham

Unless otherwise noted, Scripture text is quoted, with permission, from the New Revised Standard Version, © 1989, Division of Christian Education of the National Council of Churches of Christ in the United States of America.

To order or request information, please call 1-800-245-7894 in the U.S. or 1-800-631-6535 in Canada. Or visit www.MennoMedia.org.

17 16 15 14 13   10 9 8 7 6 5 4 3 2 1

MennoMedia
An agency of Mennonite Church USA
and Mennonite Church Canada

Kids Can Know the Way
Table of Contents

Getting Started
About the Theme

Following Jesus may seem complicated in our ever-changing world. Information is exchanged at breakneck speeds and technology is changing rapidly. So what do the stories of Jesus offer us in an information-rich world? They give us a chance to reflect on the way Jesus lived his life during his time on earth. While these lessons are geared for children, adults can just as easily benefit from stepping onto the path of Jesus' life. In each session, children will be challenged and encouraged to consider the way of Jesus and what that means for how we live today.

A thread that runs through the different settings in which people encounter Jesus is that he calls them to follow the new life he offers. Each session centers on a story of Jesus interacting with friends, new and old. As lives are changed by these encounters, so the children's lives and actions will be changed as they discover what it means to follow Jesus' way.

The prophet Isaiah had a vision of a time when the little children would lead. This is the time for children in our communities and congregations to lead the way on the path of Jesus. May their journey to know the way be a blessing to you.

About the Children

This curriculum for six- to ten-year-old children, but can be adapted for other ages. What are these children like? If you are a parent or teacher, you know that children come in all shapes and sizes. Each child is unique, and God's creativity is imprinted upon each one. **As you get to know the children as individuals, remember that children:**

- learn in different ways
- learn best by experiencing, seeing, discovering, and doing
- have differing reading abilities
- are beginning to develop abstract thinking skills
- like to move around and be active
- respond well to loving and caring adult models they can trust and follow
- like to have friends and be friendly
- can be exclusive in their friendships and often have a best friend
- have a strong sense of fairness and of right and wrong
- are already in relationship with God, even though they may not have language for their relationship
- are beginning to ask questions and need a safe environment in which to do so
- thrive when treated with love, respect, and compassion

About the Leaders

Children's experiences of faith are memorable due in part to the leaders who guide them. **Leaders who work with children:**

- model God's love, forgiveness, and care for everyone
- are mature youth or adults who always act as adults
- do not see themselves as buddies to the children, but as guides
- love children
- are energetic and enthusiastic
- have a passion for peacemaking
- have good conflict-resolution skills
- ensure that the children are safe at all times

Leaders needed for:
- **Music:** Choose songs and lead the singing.
- **Kids Know the Way:** Tell Bible stories and lead in faith conversations.
- **Kids Create:** Decide on the craft activities that will be offered, gather materials, and work with the children on a handcraft that they will take home with them. Find helpers to work with children or lead a group if you plan more than one activity.
- **Kids Move:** Lead the games and talk about how they fit with the theme.
- **Group leaders:** Build relationships with a small group of children (up to 10 children per group).
- **Memory tutors (optional):** Work one on one with children to learn memory verses.
- **Prayer pals (optional):** Pray for an individual child. An adult is matched with each child to pray for each other. Invite the pals to join you for the closing celebration.

About the Format

The curriculum:
- is geared to children in grades one through five
- can be used with multi-age groups or with separate younger and older groups
- can be adapted for kindergarten children or junior youth
- includes plans for 45–60 minute sessions
- includes time for gathering, singing, Bible story and discussion, crafts, and games
- includes ten complete sessions: kickoff session to introduce the theme, eight theme-related topics, and a final celebration event
- includes resource/reference pages with ideas for opening and closing activities, memory verses and tips for memorizing, snacks, book list, additional craft ideas, service projects, and how to manage unwanted behavior
- includes lots of suggestions for crafts and games for each session

Suggested times during each session
Kids Cluster (5 minutes)
- suggestions for early arrivals, singing, memory review

Kids Know the Way (10 minutes)
- introduction to theme, Bible story, reflection, and conversation starters

Kids Create and Kids Move (20–35 minutes)
- suggestions for activities, crafts and/or games

Closing (5 minutes), optional
- gathering time ideas for closing blessing and ending rituals

Resources

Kids Cluster

Depending upon the setup, children may arrive at a club session at different times. Be ready by having a variety of activities with which to engage children as they arrive. This helps to prevent unwanted behavior. When most of the children have arrived, or at the starting time, begin the session.

SUGGESTIONS FOR EARLY ARRIVALS

1. **Name tags:** At the first session have the children decorate their own name tags. These can be laminated and reused each session.

2. **Reading nook:** Create a place filled with various books for the children who prefer to enter into a quiet activity. Use some throw pillows for a seating area.

3. **Giant floor puzzles:** Have several available for the children who come early. Encourage the children to work in pairs or a group to solve the puzzle together.

4. **Who am I?:** Give each child a paper with the outline of a person on it and provide crayons or colored pencils. Have the children add basic things, such as hair, facial features, and clothes, to their person.

5. **Name acrostics:** Have the children write their own name vertically down the left side of a piece of paper. Then have them write a word that describes themselves that starts with each letter of their name. If the children are younger, have one of the older children help.

6. **Put the story in order:** Select a story from one of the sessions or from another source. Using simple pictures or sentences, lay out the story on several pages. Have children work together to put the story in order. Or the children can draw or write the stories as they remember them.

GROUP-BUILDING IDEAS

Children may not know each other, even if they go to the same school or church, so plan get-acquainted games.

1. **Get to know you:** Fill a grid with information such as: My eyes are brown; I have a pet; I like pizza; etc. Have the children ask each other if they match any square on the grid and, if so, to sign their copy. The children should try to get enough signatures for one row, like bingo.

2. **I like . . .:** Read a list of things that a person might like. For example: I like chocolate; I like kittens; I like pizza; I like to play outside; I like to read books; I like to go for a walk. Designate two areas, and as you read a statement, those who agree will go to one area while those who disagree will go to the other area. Continue with several statements so that the children move back and forth.

3. **Pass the message:** Use this form of the telephone game to reinforce a point from one of the lessons. Select a memory verse or a theme from a session. Divide the children into two lines and whisper the message to first child in each line. That child, in turn, whispers the message to the next person. See which team gets the message closest to the original when it reaches the end of the line.

4. **Keep them in the air:** Gather in a large area and have several balloons blown up. The children should try to keep all of the balloons in the air.

5. **Work to make the move:** Use this simple relay to help the children work together. Divide the children into two teams. At one end have a bin of shelled corn or similar object, with a scoop. Have the children use the scoop to carry the grain to an empty bin at the other end. Another variation of the game is for the children to stand in a conveyer line and pass the corn down to the other end.

6. **Walk a (short) mile:** Have the children line up in pairs and walk around the room together. Have the pairs answer a few questions, such as: What is your favorite color?, What is your favorite food?, etc. Ring a bell and have one person move forward so that new pairs are created. This may also be done with an inner circle and an outer circle.

CLOSING

This is a time to send the children out into their daily lives with a word or sentence encouraging them to remember the Bible stories at home, school, and wherever else they go. Be sure you send any announcements, crafts, and other items home with the children.

The following are closing-time suggestions:
1. Gather in a large group or plan for a simple closing at the end of the final activity.
2. Use a spoken blessing: "(Name), may Jesus be with you on the way."
3. Offer a short closing prayer.
4. Give a short blessing that is based on the session's theme (*see below*).

Sending blessings

Kickoff session: Friends of Jesus, may you learn more about him as we journey together on the path of Jesus.

Session 1: Friends of Jesus, may others be blessed as you go and proclaim the way of Jesus.

Session 2: Friends of Jesus, may you be blessed as you go and follow the call of Jesus.

Session 3: Friends of Jesus, may others be blessed as you go and share the fruit of the Spirit.

Session 4: Friends of Jesus, may you find courage as you follow Jesus' call to help others.

Session 5: Friends of Jesus, may the soil of your heart be ready for the good seeds of Jesus.

Session 6: Friends of Jesus, may you be a blessing as you share the gifts Jesus placed in you.

Session 7: Friends of Jesus, know that the Good Shepherd loves you and seeks you.

Session 8: Friends of Jesus, may all be blessed as you welcome others.

Closing celebration: Go and continue your journey on the path of Jesus!

Songs

THEME SONG:

Come and See
(*Hymnal: A Worship Book #20*)
Text and music: Marilyn Houser Hamm, based on John 1. Text and music copyright © 1974, Marilyn Houser Hamm

SONG OPTIONS:

God Loves All His Many People
(*Hymnal: A Worship Book #397*)
Text: Lubunda Mukungu: tr. Revised by Anna Juhnke
Music: Tshiluba melody (Zaire)
Mennonite World Conference Songbook, 1978

I Have Decided to Follow Jesus
(*Sing and Rejoice #39*)
Text and music: traditional

In the Bulb There Is a Flower
(*Hymnal: A Worship Book #614*)
Text and music: Natalie Sleeth
Text and music copyright © 1986 Hope Publishing Co.

Jesus, Help Us Live in Peace
(*Sing the Journey #52*)
Text and music: Gerald Derstine, based on Philippians 2:1-8
Text and music copyright © 1971, Gerald Derstine

Sizohamba Naya (We Will Walk with God)
(*Sing the Journey #78*)
Text: Swaziland traditional; transcribed by the Swedish Youth Exchange project, "Meeting Swaziland"
Music: Swaziland traditional; translated by John L. Bell
Text and music copyright © 2002 WGRG The Iona Community (Scotland)

Som'landela (We Will Follow)
(*Sing the Story #40*)
Text and music: Zimbabwean traditional

We're Following Jesus (CCLI #459571)
Text and music: Robert C. Evans
Copyright © 1990 Integrity's Hosanna! Music

Come and See

Irregular

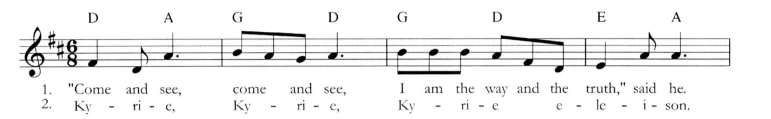

1. "Come and see, come and see, I am the way and the truth," said he.
2. Ky - ri - e, Ky - ri - e, Ky - ri - e e - le - i - son.

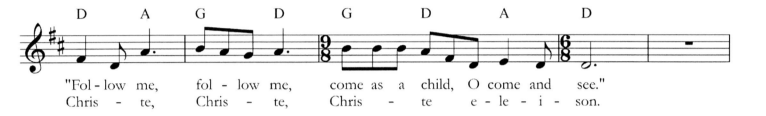

"Fol - low me, fol - low me, come as a child, O come and see."
Chris - te, Chris - te, Chris - te e - le - i - son.

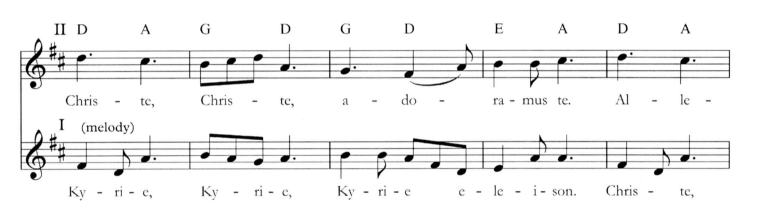

II
Chris - te, Chris - te, a - do - ra - mus te. Al - le -

I (melody)
Ky - ri - e, Ky - ri - e, Ky - ri - e e - le - i-son. Chris - te,

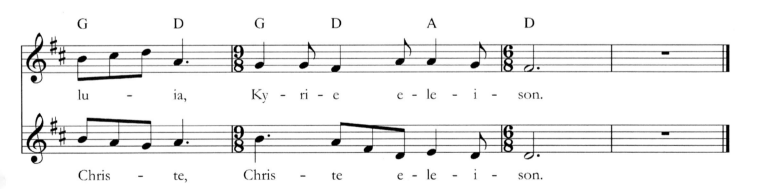

lu - ia, Ky - ri - e e - le - i - son.

Chris - te, Chris - te e - le - i - son.

* Translation: Christ, we adore you. Alleluia, Lord have mercy.
Lord, have mercy. Christ, have mercy.

Text: based on John 1, Marilyn Houser Hamm
Music: Marilyn Houser Hamm
Text and Music copyright © 1974, Marilyn Houser Hamm
Accompaniment found in *Hymnal: A Worship Book Accompaniment Handbook*

Bible memory verses & tips

If Bible memory is important for your club, find time each session to practice the memory verses.

Learn the texts over the course of the sessions, and spend time each session reviewing a section of verses. Send copies of the memory verses home and encourage children to learn them between sessions.

Choose a time to practice the memory texts: during the snack, during gathering time, before the Bible story, during craft time, or as part of the sending.

The following are Bible memory options:

Kickoff session: Make me to know your ways, O Lord; teach me your paths (Psalm 25:4).

Session 1: The Spirit of the Lord is upon me, because he has anointed me to bring good news to the poor (Luke 4:18a).

Session 2: Follow me, and I will make you fish for people (Matthew 4:19b).

Session 3: You will know them by their fruits (Matthew 7:20).

Session 4: We have never seen anything like this (Mark 2:12b)!

Session 5: The seed is the word of God (Luke 8:11b).

Session 6: And all ate and were filled (Mark 6:42).

Session 7: Rejoice with me, for I have found my sheep that was lost (Luke 15:6b).

Session 8: Martha welcomed him into her home (Luke 10:38b).

FUN WAYS TO MEMORIZE SCRIPTURE

1. **Play a game using flash cards.** Use one card for each word of a Bible verse. Distribute the cards to the children. Ask them to line up holding their cards in the proper order.
2. **Place the flash cards on a wall.** Children remove one word at a time and repeat the entire verse until all the cards are gone.
3. **Create hand motions** to key words.
4. **Say the verse while doing different actions** (running on the spot, hopping on one foot, doing stride jumps, marching).
5. **Stand or sit in a circle** and assign phrases or words for each child or small group to repeat. Continue until everyone knows the verse.
6. **Balloon tap:** Children tap a balloon in the air each time they say a word in the verse.
7. **Ball throw:** Children throw a ball to each other as they say the next word in the verse.
8. **Use rhythm instruments** and chant the text.
9. **Invite the children to illustrate key words** and use the pictures as memory aids.
10. **Repeat memory verses often in a variety of settings.** Do it while the children eat, when they gather, while they work on a craft or play a game, or at the end of the session.

Note
....
Feel free to use a different Bible translation if you prefer.

Book List

Set up a mini-library with books related to the theme. Check with your church, school, or public librarian for these and other books. Children may look at books when they have extra time during the session.

1.   Bozzuti-Jones, Mark Francisco. *Jesus the Word*. Minneapolis: Augsburg Books, 2005.
2.   Butterworth, Nick and Mick Inkpen. *Lost Sheep*. New York: Harper Collins, 1994.
3.   Henry, Kim and Mary Anne Lard. *Seeds of Heaven*. New York: Morehouse Publishing, 2000.
4.   Hoffman, Mary. *Miracles: Wonders Jesus Worked*. New York: Penguin Putman, 2001.
5.   Meyer, Mary Clemens. *Walking with Jesus: Stories about Real People who Return Good for Evil*. Scottdale, PA: Herald Press, 1992.
6.   Osborne, Rick and K. Christie Bowler. *I Want to Know About the Fruit of the Spirit*. Grand Rapids: Zondervan, 1999.
7.   Paterson, Katherine. *The Light of the World: The Life of Jesus for Children*. New York: Scholastic, 2008.
8.   Pingry, Patricia A. *The Story of Jesus*. Nashville, TN: Ideals Publications, 2006.
9.   Weaver, Lisa D. *Praying with Our Feet*. Scottdale, PA: Herald Press, 2005.

Snacks

Suggestions are given for general snacks and for specific snacks to use in various sessions. Be aware of food allergies. It is best not to use nuts or nut products.

GENERAL SNACK IDEAS

- Dried fruit of any kind: apricots, raisins, Craisins
- Fresh fruit: apples, grapes, orange slices, bananas
- Popcorn or popcorn balls
- Yogurt parfaits: yogurt layered with fruit and granola
- Vegetables and dip: carrots, celery, cucumbers, broccoli, cauliflower

KICKOFF SESSION

Make a snack mix of peanuts, raisins, M&M's, and pretzels.

SESSION 1

Peanut Butter Rollups: Spread a small flour or corn tortilla with a peanut butter and honey mixture. Offer different toppings, such as chocolate chips, raisins, granola, and jelly, for the children to top their peanut butter with. Roll the tortillas up and cut them into bite-sized pieces.

SESSION 2

Deviled Egg Boats: Make deviled eggs. Cut triangle shapes out of red or orange peppers and place one triangle on each egg to make a sail.

SESSION 3

Make Kindness Kabobs (page 33, a Kids Create activity) or Frozen Fruit Slushies (page 34, a Kids Move activity).

SESSION 4

Mini Sandwiches: Cut cheese and meat into the shape of a cracker, layer together, and serve as mini sandwiches.

SESSION 5

Enjoy edible seeds, such as roasted pumpkin seeds, sunflower seeds, a variety of nuts, and toasted soybeans.

SESSION 6

Bring items for Mixed-up Picnic (page 48, a Kids Move activity) or make Marshmallow Popcorn Treats: Melt marshmallows and butter in the microwave. Coat the popcorn with the marshmallow mixture and form into small balls that fit inside a muffin tin.

SESSION 7

Apple Sandwiches: Core an apple and cut it into rings. Spread one ring with peanut butter or cream cheese, add some raisins, and top it with a second ring.

SESSION 8

Serve pretzels, crackers, cheese, grapes, bananas, carrots, and M&Ms for Hospitality Café (page 60, a Kids Move activity).

CLOSING CELEBRATION

Veggie Flowers: Provide cucumbers, carrots, celery, radishes, cherry tomatoes, and dip. Have children and adults make their own flower creations to eat.

Extended craft projects

Each session includes a variety of craft ideas. Some children, especially older ones, enjoy working on a larger project that extends over a number of weeks. Instead of choosing a craft for each session, you may wish to choose a craft that extends for several sessions.

KNOW THE WAY MURAL

A mural will help the children visualize their journey along the way. Begin the mural during the kickoff session and add to it each week to serve as a visual record of stories learned.

Stretch a large sheet of paper on the floor. Draw a path on the paper and allow the children to carefully walk along the path. As part of the closing activities, invite the children to draw pictures along one side of the path to illustrate the Bible story that was presented.

Encourage the children to think about how the story applies to their own lives. Some may want to draw pictures on the other side of the path that illustrate ways they have "known the way" in their own lives.

If this series is hosted by a congregation, invite members to add their own stories and illustrations to the mural, showing ways that they have followed Jesus.

WALKING WITH JESUS

Footprints will represent the children walking with Jesus as they learn to know the way. In preparation, make a number of footprints of various sizes and colors of construction paper. Display them in a main gathering area or hallway that leads to the meeting space. Prior to each session, add a sign with the name of that session.

At the kickoff session, invite each child and adult to select a footprint, write his or her name on it, and place it at the beginning of the hallway or gathering area.

After each session, invite children and adults to select another footprint and write down one detail they remember from the Bible story. Add these to the area underneath each session's sign. Congregational members can add their footprints as well, using different colors of feet.

After the closing celebration, children may collect their footprints to remind them of all they learned.

Note

Be aware of children who are in a wheelchair or who use crutches. They may want to use tracks instead of footprints. Give them a choice about how they would like to leave their imprint.

Tips on Managing Unwanted Behavior

- **Be prepared.** Give yourself time to read through the session and prepare. Be in the meeting area early so you are ready to greet the children as they arrive. The session begins the minute the first child arrives!

- **Be consistent.** Create, display, and review guidelines for how the group behaves together, and remind children of expectations often. Stop the session and address unwanted behavior as often as necessary so the children know you are serious about expectations.

- **Be observant.** Observe the different abilities and interests of each child. Keep the session active. Engage children's minds and bodies as you teach. As often as possible, let the children move around. For example, use actions with songs and memory work, sit on floor for the Bible story, and stand at a table for crafts.

- **Be encouraging.** Reinforce positive behaviors in affirming, spoken ways. Wait until everyone is quiet and attentive before beginning instructions. Speak clearly and slowly, making sure everyone understands what is being said.

- **Be ready to apologize.** If you have made a mistake, apologize to the child or group. This can be a teachable moment as you model what it means to be a peacemaker.

- **Be a leader, not a buddy.** Let the children know you care about them, but relate to them as a leader. Children respect you more when they know what to expect from you.

- **Seek help from others.** Ask an adult to give extra attention to any child with behavioral challenges. Seek counsel from other leaders and parents. If you do not know how to handle a discipline challenge, talk to someone who can help you.

- **Pray.** Pray that each child may experience God's love and peace, especially while in your care.

- **Choose to love each child unconditionally** regardless of his or her behavior.

- **Practice peacemaking** and conflict-resolution skills at all times.

Kickoff Session
Begin on the Way

This session sets the stage for the sessions to come by showing that as a young child Jesus needed to be in God's house.

Jesus was raised in the local synagogue and was well aware of the Scriptures. It was clear from his interaction with the temple officials in Jerusalem that he had learned well. Encourage the children that they are not too young to learn the ways of Jesus.

The memory verse is Psalm 25:4: Make me to know your ways, O Lord; teach me your paths.

BIBLE TEXT
Luke 2:39-52

FAITH CHALLENGE
We can learn about God, just like Jesus did.

ADVANCE PREPARATION
- Read through the entire session and decide what you will do.
- Set up the space for the various activities.
- Practice the theme song or other music you may wish to sing.
- Gather supplies for the activities you choose to do.
- Prepare a snack (p. 12).
- Identify two familiar points that are a short distance apart. Identify other locations that are about 120 miles / 193 kilometers apart and that would be familiar to the children.

Kids Cluster

1. **Plan an activity for early arrivals.** Check page 6 for ideas.
2. **If the children do not know each other,** make name tags and play some get-acquainted games (p. 6).
3. **Welcome the children and gather for a time of singing** (p. 8). Be sure to include action songs, familiar songs, favorite songs, and new songs.
4. **Talk with the children about a trip they have taken.** How did they prepare? What kinds of things did they take along? Were there things they wanted to take along but were not able to? Have them share about their trips, whether a day trip such as a field trip or an extended family vacation.

15

Kids Know the Way ...

1. **Begin by singing the theme song,** "Come and See" (p. 9).

2. **Introduce the theme of the day:** We can learn about God, just like Jesus did.

3. **Ask the children how they made the trip to be together** at Kids Can today. Some of them will have come by car; others may have walked or ridden their bikes. Ask them how they think Jesus got around in his day: Did he have a car to drive or a bike to ride? Explain that when Jesus and his family wanted to get around, they mostly had to walk. They might have used a donkey, but if they needed to go somewhere they generally had to use their feet. Today in the story we will learn about a time when Jesus and his family went to the city of Jerusalem. Each year Jesus and his family walked 120 miles / 193 kilometers to Jerusalem.

4. **Open your Bible to Luke 2:39-52,** and either read or retell it in your own words.

5. **Talk about the different parts of the story.** Ask the children:
   - How did Jesus' parents react to him staying behind in the temple?
   - How would your parents react if you stayed behind without their permission?
   - Why was it important to Jesus to be in the temple?
   - What did the leaders have to say about Jesus?

Kids Create

LEARN AT THE TEMPLE
(INDIVIDUAL)

Materials: copies of Deuteronomy 6:4-6, paper, crayons, markers

When children were young in Jesus' time, they learned to read and write at the synagogue in their hometown. They would learn about the Scriptures and about God. One of the first Scriptures they learned was Deuteronomy 6:4-6.

- Invite children to make their own copy of the verse. Replace words with symbols to make it easier to remember.

  hear—draw an ear
  love—draw a heart
  soul—draw hands over heart
  might—draw strong arms
  keep—draw a treasure box
  heart—draw a heart

TRAVEL TO THE TEMPLE
(GROUP AND INDIVIDUAL)

Materials: map from Jesus' time (p. 19), maps of your local area, crayons

- Review together the trip that Jesus and his family made to the temple. Look on the map to see the path Jesus would have taken from his hometown of Nazareth to the city of Jerusalem. Mark it with a crayon.
- Give each child a map of the local area and point out the path from your current location to another destination in the area. If children live in the area, they may want to follow the path to their house. Have each child use a crayon and mark the path.

MAKE AN IMPRINT
(PAIRS AND INDIVIDUAL)

Materials: copy paper or a variety of colors of construction paper, pencils, scissors, crayons or markers, a copy of the memory verse

- Assign the children into pairs, making sure all of the younger children are working with an older child.
- The children will remove one shoe and then take turns tracing their partner's foot onto a piece of paper. This works best on a hard surface floor.
- Each child will cut out the tracing of his or her own foot.
- The children will copy the memory verse onto their footprints.
- Encourage them to take the footprint home and place it somewhere they can see it every day. It will remind them of the journey with Jesus that they are taking over the next nine weeks.

Kids Move

PACK FOR THE JOURNEY RELAY
(GROUP)
Materials: two backpacks filled with these or similar items: shirt, jeans, socks, flashlight, map, food containers, spoon, fork, plastic cup, jacket, small pillow, small blanket, teddy bear

- In preparation, create a starting line on the floor. Place the backpacks at the opposite side of the starting line, with the items laid out next to the backpacks. Divide the children into two teams.
- Have the teams begin together at the starting line.
- The first person goes to the opposite end, fills the backpack with the items, runs with the backpack to the start line, and gives it to the next child.
- The next child runs to the opposite end, empties the backpack, runs back to the start, and tags the next child.
- Continue until everyone has had a turn.

TRAVEL TO THE TEMPLE
(GROUP)
Materials: whistle or bell, snack

Jesus and his family made a long trek from their hometown to Jerusalem; it would have taken them many days.

- Take a walk to demonstrate what it is like to walk with a group.
- Have the children walk with a partner and talk about what they did that day.
- When you signal with the bell or whistle, have the children change partners.
- Take your snack with you and have a break for meals.

WHERE IS JESUS?
(PAIRS)
Materials: signs that are numbered and say "Jesus" along with a Bible verse (see suggestions, page 20), paper, pencils, Bibles

- In preparation, hang the signs in many places, some obvious and some hidden, around the building.
- Children will work in pairs to find Jesus all around the building.
- Each pair will record the number on the sign and where they found it.
- Give a time limit and ring the bell to gather together when the time is up.
- Children will look up their verses and share them with the group to hear words that Jesus spoke.

CLOSER TO GOD
(PAIRS)
Materials: One yard- or one meter-length of string for each pair, beads

- Children will line up in two lines facing each other. Those across from each other will be partners.
- Give a string to each pair. Each person will hold one end and move as far apart as they can while still holding the string tight.
- Give one child in each pair a bead. He or she will need to thread the bead on the string.
- The partners need to pass the bead to each other without touching it. They should adapt the string length with each pass and note that as they get closer to each other, it is easier to pass the bead.
- Remind children that the closer they are to Jesus, the easier it is to see him in their lives.

Closing
For closing ideas, see page 7.

SUGGESTED VERSES FOR WHERE IS JESUS?

MATTHEW

3:17: And a voice from heaven said, "This is my Son, the Beloved, with whom I am well pleased."

6:11: Give us this day our daily bread.

26:36: Then Jesus went with them to a place called Gethsemane; and he said to his disciples, "Sit here while I go over there and pray."

MARK

2:14: As he was walking along, he saw Levi son of Alphaeus sitting at the tax booth, and he said to him, "Follow me." And he got up and followed him.

4:39: He woke up and rebuked the wind, and said to the sea, "Peace! Be still!" Then the wind ceased, and there was a dead calm.

6:31: He said to them, "Come away to a deserted place all by yourselves and rest a while." For many were coming and going, and they had no leisure even to eat.

LUKE

2:49: He said to them, "Why were you searching for me? Did you not know that I must be in my Father's house?"

12:28: But if God so clothes the grass of the field, which is alive today and tomorrow is thrown into the oven, how much more will he clothe you—you of little faith!

18:16: But Jesus called for them and said, "Let the little children come to me, and do not stop them; for it is to such as these that the kingdom of God belongs."

JOHN

1:39: He said to them, "Come and see." They came and saw where he was staying, and they remained with him that day.

5:8: Jesus said to him, "Stand up, take your mat and walk."

6:20: But he said to them, "It is I; do not be afraid."

Session 1
Learn from the Teacher

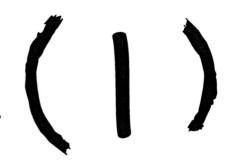

Jesus proclaimed that the Spirit of the Lord was upon him to bring the good news. Jesus was not taken seriously in his hometown. The people who heard Jesus make the proclamation had known him since he was a child. They watched him grow up, and now he was presenting himself as the Messiah, the one anointed by God to bring the good news of release for the captives, sight for the blind, and freedom for the oppressed. Jesus was bold in his declarations to the people gathered there, letting them know they were in need of this message as well.

This lesson should encourage the children to think about the ways they hear the voice of Jesus and follow his ways, and how they can invite others to know the way.

The memory verse is Luke 4:18a: The Spirit of the Lord is upon me, because he has anointed me to bring good news to the poor.

BIBLE TEXT
Luke 4:14-30, 42-44
(additional text: Mark 6:1-6)

FAITH CHALLENGE
Jesus shows us how to proclaim the way.

ADVANCE PREPARATION
- Read through the entire session and decide what you will do.
- Set up the space for the various activities.
- Practice the theme song or other music you may wish to sing.
- Gather supplies for the activities you choose to do.
- Prepare a snack (p. 12).
- Prepare cards with printed texts to be read aloud in the Kids Cluster section (Isaiah 58:6; Isaiah 61:1-2; Mark 6:1-6).

Kids Cluster

1. **Plan an activity for early arrivals.** Check page 6 for ideas.
2. **If the children do not know each other,** make name tags and play some get-acquainted games (p. 6).
3. **Welcome the children and gather for a time of singing** (p. 8). Be sure to include action songs, familiar songs, favorite songs, and new songs.
4. **Invite children who are comfortable to read a text printed on a card.** Be aware that some children will not feel comfortable reading to the group.

Kids Know the Way ...

1. **Begin by singing the theme song,** "Come and See" (p. 9).
2. **Introduce the theme of the day:** Jesus shows us how to proclaim the way.
3. **Explain that in today's story Jesus is going to the synagogue in his hometown.** For us this would be like going to the local church. Each time they met on the Sabbath, Scripture, from what is our Old Testament, was read. Jesus was at the synagogue, as was normal for him, but on that day he read a Scripture passage that told the people gathered that he was the One sent by God to show the way to God.
4. **Open the Bible to Luke 4:14-30, 42-44,** and either read or retell it in your own words.
5. **Talk with the children about knowing when God comes to us.** Ask them:
   - Where does God come to us?
   - How does God come to us?
   - What were some of the things that Jesus was saying to the people in the synagogue?
   - What did you hear Jesus saying to you?
   - How will others know we are following Jesus?

Kids Create

NEWS REPORT
(PAIRS OR SMALL GROUPS)

Materials: list of interview questions (see below), biblical-era dress/costumes, video camera

Have the children work together in small groups to prepare a news report based on the story in Luke 4:14-30. This could include an interview with Jesus or someone who was in the crowd. Dress the children in costumes if the interviews are recorded. The recordings can be shared at the closing celebration.

Sample questions for the interview: Who was preaching here today? What text did he use? What did he say about the text? What did you think as you heard him talking? How did the crowd respond? What did you do? What do you think will happen to Jesus next?

TAKE THE WORD
(INDIVIDUAL)

Materials: two pencils or round chopsticks for each child, pens or pencils, parchment paper, yarn, tape

- Have the children write Luke 4:18a onto a piece of paper. If there are younger children, you may want to have the verse printed on the page for them to trace, or you may want to have them write a smaller selection.
- Help the children use tape to attach a chopstick or pencil to the top and bottom edges of the paper.
- Roll the paper up to the middle and tie with a string. Explain that people in Jesus' day would have read from type of scroll instead of from a bound book.

PLAN A WORSHIP SERVICE
(INDIVIDUAL OR GROUP)

Materials: samples of printed order of service, list of suggested Scripture passages, list of suggested songs

There was form and structure to the worship service that Jesus attended, just as there is similar form and structure to our worship services today. A simple order is: reading from the law and prophets (Old Testament), reciting Scripture from memory, prayer, sermon or teaching, shared praises or singing.

- In preparation, identify a few Scripture passages that are frequently used for worship. Identify music and songs that are used during worship.
- Allow the children to plan a worship service following the simple order named above. They may choose children to lead various parts of the service.

The service may be shared during the closing celebration.

Kids Move

FIVE SENSES TOUR
(GROUP)

Materials: chart paper, marker

- Divide the children into five groups. Assign one of the five senses—touch, smell, sight, taste, and hearing—to each group.
- Have each group go on a walk around the area and note what they experienced using only that one sense.
- When all the groups return, have each report on what they experienced. Record the responses on chart paper.
- Be aware of children, friends, and family members who might not be able to use all of their senses. How do they experience the world?
- Encourage the children to use all of their senses as they are able as they look for God in the world around them and as they follow the way of Jesus.

RELEASE TAG
(GROUP)

- Identify one child to be Jesus. Divide the rest of the children into two groups.
- One group will form pairs. Their objective is to capture someone from the other group by joining hands around that person.
- When Jesus touches a child held inside the pair, the child is set free.
- Once children are set free, they may free other children as well.
- Play again, identifying a new person as Jesus and changing the groups.

WHO IS CALLING?
(GROUP)

- Divide the children into two groups. Place them at opposite ends of a large space, facing opposite directions.
- Identify a caller on one side to say, "The Spirit of the Lord is upon me."
- Prepare the other group to receive the message with their eyes closed.
- After the caller has made the statement, give the other side a chance to identify the speaker.
- Take turns using callers from each side.

Closing

For closing ideas, see page 7.

Session 2
Follow the Call

The call to follow Jesus can be complicated to explain to younger children. Based on their life experiences, it may be easier for them to understand the concept of their name being called, leaving their things behind, and following up on a request from an adult.

Jesus called the disciples out of their daily work to follow him. We often think of the call to follow as an individual call, which it is, but it is also important to note that Jesus called people to be a part of a larger group. Texts from Luke and Mark are used in this lesson to emphasize the use of the disciples' names.

The memory verse is Matthew 4:19b: Follow me, and I will make you fish for people.

BIBLE TEXT
Luke 5:1-11
Mark 3:13-19

FAITH CHALLENGE
We can follow Jesus' call.

ADVANCE PREPARATION
- Read through the entire session and decide what you will do.
- Set up the space for the various activities.
- Practice the theme song or other music you may wish to sing.
- Gather supplies for the activities you choose to do.
- Prepare a snack (p. 12).

Kids Cluster

1. **Plan an activity for early arrivals.** Check page 6 for ideas.
2. **Welcome the children and gather for a time of singing** (p. 8).
3. **Talk with the children about names.** Ask them:
   - Do you have a nickname? Is there a special name you have for someone else?
   - Do different people say your name differently at different times? (For example, a parent may use a child's full name when the parent wants the child's attention.)
   - What does it feel like when someone calls your name?
   - How does it feel when you hear your name used by someone special?

Kids Know the Way . . .

1. **Begin by singing the theme song,** "Come and See" (p. 9).

2. **Introduce the theme of the day:** We can follow Jesus' call.

3. **Open your Bible to Luke 5:1-11, then Mark 3:13-19.** Explain that in today's lesson Jesus is starting his ministry and is calling others to follow him, and that there are stories that tell us about this. Read or retell the stories from Luke and Mark.

4. **Talk about the different parts of the story.** Ask the children:

   - Do you wonder if the men Jesus called knew who he was before he called their names?
   - How do you think they felt about Jesus calling them by name?
   - Would you have been ready to follow Jesus like the disciples were?
   - What does it mean to be called by Jesus to be his followers?
   - How do we follow Jesus every day?

Kids Create

HOW WE FOLLOW JESUS
(INDIVIDUAL)

Materials: large sheets of construction paper, regular-sized sheets of construction paper, fish cutouts (p. 29), glue, scissors

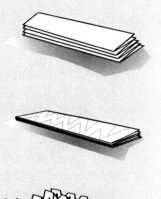

- Have the children select one large sheet and one regular-sized sheet of construction paper. They will fold the regular-sized sheet accordion style.
- Show the children how to cut out triangles along the top and bottom of the folded construction paper. Younger children will need help cutting. When opened, this becomes the net.
- Glue the net to the larger paper.
- Give each child some fish cutouts or have the children trace a template and cut their own.
- Brainstorm ways we can follow Jesus. (Examples: help a friend, share toys, be kind, listen to parents, laugh with each other, offer comfort.) Have the children write some of these ideas onto the fish. Put the fish into the nets.
- Write "How we follow Jesus" at the top of the paper.

FISH NETS
(INDIVIDUAL)

Materials: heavy string or yarn—you will need 30 18-in. / 46-cm. pieces of heavy string or yarn and one 4-ft. / 1.2-m piece for each net

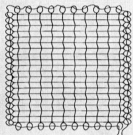

- Children will tie a small loop at each end of every short piece of string. Younger children may need help. Pieces now measure 12 in / 30.5 cm.
- Lay 20 of the pieces parallel to each other and weave the remaining 10 pieces into the 20.
- After all 10 pieces are woven through, take the longer piece of yarn and thread it through the loops on the ends of each piece.
- Lay the net flat, then string it up to catch fish.
- These are small individual nets. You may make a very large net as a group to use in the Fish in the Net game (Kids Move).

WE EACH DO OUR PART
(PAIRS)

Materials: people cut-outs (p. 30), paper, glue, pencils or pens, crayons or markers

- Talk with the children about how we each do our part to follow Jesus. We follow Jesus individually and as a group. Ask the children: How do people work together to follow Jesus?
- Give each pair a blank piece of paper and people cutouts. Have children glue the cutouts to illustrate a story of working together to follow Jesus. They may include a short written story as well and then add color to the illustrations.

Display these for adults to review at the closing celebration.

Kids Move

FISH IN THE NET
(GROUP)

Materials: large fish net, many blown-up balloons

- Gather the children in a large area. Place the large fish net in the middle and assign two or three children to hold the corners of the net.
- Scatter the balloons around the area.
- The children not holding the net will gather the balloons and put them in the net. There should be enough balloons to make it difficult to get all of them in the net.
- After the balloons have been gathered, those holding the net should send them flying.
- Remind the children that as followers of Jesus we are called to go and share Jesus' story.

Send a balloon home with each child as a reminder that we are called to follow Jesus' way.

Closing
For closing ideas, see page 7.

SARDINES
(GROUP)

Explain that just as Jesus gathers people together, we will gather together in this game.

- Designate one child to hide.
- Explain that the object of the game is to find the person who is hiding and wait with him or her until everyone is hiding together.
- While the child is hiding, count aloud to 50 before allowing the other children to silently search for the one who is hidden.
- The person who is the last to find the group is the first person to hide the next time.

FOLLOW THE CALL
(GROUP)

- Designate one child to be the leader.
- Have the other children spread out around the room or in an open space.
- The leader goes to one of the other children, says the child's name, and asks him or her to follow.
- They form a chain and go to the next child until all the children have been called by name and have joined the chain.

Session 3
Bear Good Fruit

Jesus builds this parable from life in his homeland. There was good farmland in the valley near the Sea of Galilee, but there were also areas of desert and soil that were very rocky and not suited for crops. Famers in the local villages farmed on small plots located outside of the villages.

People in Jesus' time understood that trees in good soil would produce a good product. In the same way, they understood that trees in bad soil would produce bad fruit. While this concept may be difficult for the children to understand, the expression of bearing good fruit connected to the fruits of the Spirit is a good way to give them tangible expressions of following Jesus.

The memory verse is Matthew 7:20: You will know them by their fruits.

BIBLE TEXT
Matthew 7:15-20
Luke 6:43-45
(additional text: Galatians 5:22-23)

FAITH CHALLENGE
We can grow good fruit.

ADVANCE PREPARATION
- Read through the entire session and decide what you will do.
- Set up the space for the various activities.
- Practice the theme song or other music you may wish to sing.
- Gather supplies for the activities you choose to do.
- Prepare a snack (p. 12).
- Gather various fruit—overripe, underripe, ripe, and plastic—in a bowl.

Kids Cluster

1. **Plan an activity for early arrivals.** Check page 6 for ideas.
2. **Welcome the children and gather for a time of singing** (p. 8). Be sure to include action songs, familiar songs, favorite songs, and new songs.
3. **Show the bowl of fruit with the different types of fruit in it.** Pass it around and allow the children to touch and smell the fruit. Tell the children that the story is about following Jesus by bearing fruit. Trees that grow in good soil and receive the right amounts of sun and rain will produce good fruit. Trees that grow in poor soil and do not receive the right amounts of sun and rain will not produce good fruit. As people, we need to grow in Jesus so that we produce good fruit in our own lives.

Kids Know the Way ...

1. **Begin by singing the theme song,** "Come and See" (p. 9).

2. **Introduce the theme of the day:** We can grow good fruit.

3. **Open your Bible to Matthew 7:15-20 and Luke 6:43-45.** Tell the children that today's Bible stories are parables. Sometimes Jesus used common examples to explain difficult topics, and these stories are called parables. Today's difficult topic is about fruit growing in us, so Jesus talked about the common example of a fruit tree. In the stories, Jesus told his disciples about fruit that we produce when we follow Jesus. When we follow Jesus, our lives produce good fruit. Read or retell the stories.

4. **Talk with the children about the different parts of the story.** Ask them:
   - Can you name different kinds of fruit that grow on trees? Which are your favorites to eat?
   - What do we need in our lives to bear good fruit?
   - How can we show that we are growing good fruit?

5. **Tell the children that it is sometimes difficult to talk about us giving fruit,** so the Bible includes helpful verses so that we can know what good fruit looks like. In Galatians 5:22-23, we find out that good fruit is love, joy, peace, patience, kindness, generosity, faithfulness, gentleness, and self-control. These are known as the fruits of the Spirit.

6. **Read the list again, slowly this time,** and ask for examples of actions that demonstrate the fruits of the Spirit.

Kids Create

FRUIT OF THE SPIRIT TREE
(INDIVIDUAL)

Materials: paper, crayons, fruit shapes (p. 35), glue

- Give the children paper and invite them to draw a tree that looks like a person. (Example: Have them start with drawing a simple figure of themselves with their arms as branches and their body as a trunk. Their hair could be more leafy green branches.)
- Give them fruit shapes to represent the good fruit of the Spirit.
- Have them write the name of good fruits onto the fruit shapes and glue them to the tree.

KINDNESS KABOBS
(PAIRS AND GROUP)

Materials: wooden skewers, eight different kinds of fruit (one for each fruit of the Spirit), fruit dip

- Place bowls of fruit on tables in an open area.
- Pair children to help each other gather their fruit, two pieces of each kind for each pair.
- Have them work together, side by side or across the table. One person holds a skewer while the other places one piece of each kind of fruit on it. Then they switch positions and fill the other skewer.
- Offer fruit dip and enjoy!

FRUIT SEARCH
(INDIVIDUAL)

Materials: copies of the word search on page 36, pencils

- Invite the children to find the fruits and fruits of the Spirit in the word search.

Kids Move

GATHER THE FRUIT SCAVENGER HUNT
(SMALL GROUPS)
Materials: prepared fruit shapes (p. 35), basket for each group, clues or map if desired

- In preparation, make different fruit shapes for each fruit of the Spirit, enough for each small group. Hide all the shapes of each type of fruit in a different place. For example, hide all the apples in one place, all the bananas in another place, etc. Create clues or a map to help find the fruit, if desired.
- Divide children into groups of three or four and give each group a basket.
- Send them around the area to search for the fruit. You may give them a set of clues or a map to help find the fruit.
- After they have collected each kind of fruit, each group will return to the common area to make sure they have one of each type.

ADDITIONAL OPTION FOR SNACK
FROZEN FRUIT SLUSHIES
Ahead of time, make easy Frozen Fruit Slushies: Mix one can of orange juice concentrate with two cups of sugar. Add three cups of water and a variety of crushed fruit: bananas, oranges, pineapple, grapes, strawberries, peaches, and blueberries. The amount of the fruit needed is based on how many different kinds you use. Pour into individual cups and freeze. Let thaw for about an hour before serving.

Closing
For closing ideas, see page 7.

ACT OUT THE FRUITS
(PAIRS AND GROUP)
Materials: a list of the fruits of the Spirit for each group

- Divide children into pairs and give each pair a fruit of the Spirit.
- Invite children to think about how they can act out their fruit.
- Present the acting to the whole group and have others guess the fruit.

Additional idea: Each group could act out a fruit of the Spirit and its opposite.

FRUIT TASTING
(GROUP)
Materials: eight different types of fruit, napkins

- In preparation, place the different fruit in a covered bowl.
- Give each fruit, one at a time, to each child. As they eat, say a bit about the fruit to reinforce the sweetness of bearing good fruit in their lives.

Examples:
Love: strawberry—shaped like a heart
Joy: banana—looks like a smile
Peace: watermelon or cantaloupe—needs to be eaten one piece at a time
Patience: orange—needs to be peeled
Kindness: grapes—easy to share
Generosity: apple—sweet flavor
Faithfulness: pear—texture of life
Gentleness: peach or nectarine—soft outside
Self-control: kiwi—rough outside but worthwhile inside

BANANA

ORANGE

KIWI

STRAWBERRY

GRAPES

PINEAPPLE

APPLE

PEAR

LEMON

FRUIT WORD SEARCH

Find these words:

APPLE	GRAPES	LEMON	PEACE
FAITHFULNESS	JOY	LOVE	PEAR
GENEROSITY	KINDNESS	MANGO	PLUM
GENTLENESS	KIWI	PATIENCE	SELF CONTROL

```
R  U  V  L  O  B  P  K  I  N  D  N  E  S  S
C  P  I  G  N  X  Y  E  F  D  S  O  L  B  R
G  E  N  E  R  O  S  I  T  Y  I  C  T  D  P
R  M  U  N  A  T  S  Y  W  P  N  F  S  Z  A
A  I  B  T  L  M  Y  C  Z  O  P  S  E  K  T
P  A  R  L  E  M  O  N  H  G  E  E  L  Y  I
E  T  W  E  J  E  L  B  S  N  A  I  F  T  E
S  M  A  N  G  O  M  R  L  U  R  F  C  B  N
W  L  Y  E  Q  T  K  U  D  O  L  E  O  Y  C
S  P  R  S  W  I  F  M  I  T  V  S  N  U  E
R  U  D  S  L  H  Y  G  R  P  D  E  T  O  G
I  J  Z  O  T  L  C  R  N  I  V  Y  R  P  L
K  I  W  I  T  U  Y  I  V  D  H  J  O  Y  O
J  T  A  P  P  L  E  O  P  N  E  P  L  U  M
Y  F  B  C  N  P  E  A  C  E  D  M  P  A  R
```

Session 4
Help a Friend

Oftentimes a lesson from this biblical text will focus on the healing or the sins being forgiven. These are very important parts of the lesson and should be highlighted. However, for this lesson the focus is on the friends and how they worked together to get their mutual friend to Jesus.

These friends were very determined to do what they could to get their friend to Jesus, even it if meant removing a section of the roof of a house to ensure that their friend was able to see Jesus. Encourage the children to think about the ways they have been good friends and the ways their actions and their words have shown that they follow Jesus.

The memory verse is Mark 2:12b: We have never seen anything like this!

BIBLE TEXT
Mark 2:3-12
(additional texts: Matthew 9:2-8, Luke 5:18-26)

FAITH CHALLENGE
Jesus calls us to help others.

ADVANCE PREPARATION
- Read through the entire session and decide what you will do.
- Set up the space for the various activities.
- Practice the theme song or other music you may wish to sing.
- Gather supplies for the activities you choose to do.
- Prepare a snack (p. 12).
- Gather pictures of people who help others (firefighter, nurse, clerk, etc.), pictures of adults in your church helping others, and a mirror.

Kids Cluster

1. **Plan an activity for early arrivals.** Check page 6 for ideas.
2. **Welcome the children and gather for a time of singing** (p. 8). Be sure to include action songs, familiar songs, favorite songs, and new songs.
3. **Show pictures of people who are helpers.** Talk about the ways we help each other and ask the children to share examples of helping someone. Make a connection between people who help others and the ways we follow Jesus by helping others with small things. Share pictures of people from your congregation helping others.
4. **Ask: Who can help others?** Hold up a mirror, allowing the children to see themselves. Remind the children that they are friends who can help friends.

Kids Know the Way . . .

1. **Begin by singing the theme song,** "Come and See" (p. 9).
2. **Introduce the theme of the day:** Jesus calls us to help others.
3. **Open your Bible to Mark 2:3-12.** Tell the children that they will hear a story about friends who went out of their way to make sure their friend received the help he needed. These friends wanted to get their friend to Jesus, and the way they made that happen is surprising. Sometimes friends need to be creative to help a friend in need. Read or retell the story.
4. **Talk with the children about the different parts of the story.** Ask them:
   - How do you think the owner of the house reacted when a man was being lowered down from the roof? (Be sure to point out to the children that houses then were constructed differently than modern homes are.)
   - Why did the friends bring the paralyzed man to Jesus?
   - How did the man respond to Jesus healing him?
   - Why did Jesus heal people?

Kids Create

THROUGH THE ROOF
(INDIVIDUAL)

Materials: a shoebox or other box of similar size for each child, scissors, small canvas or burlap rectangles, string, hole punch, markers or crayons, clay

- Close the boxes and have each child draw a rectangle on the lid. Have adults assist the children in cutting out the rectangles.
- Have the children decorate the box to look like a house. They can use the clay to make small people: the healed man, the four friends, and Jesus.
- After the houses are complete, children can use their set and canvas rectangle to retell the story.

BE AN ENCOURAGER
(INDIVIDUAL)

Materials: card stock cut to size, envelopes, markers, stickers, crayons, pencils

- In preparation, set up a station for the children to make cards with encouraging messages to give to their friends. If there is time, they can make more than one card.
- Include sample messages, such as: I like having you for a friend. You did a great thing. Hope you get better soon. I really liked it when you (fill in the blank). Thanks for helping me out.
- Allow the children to use their creativity when creating their card(s). They may copy one of the sample messages or write their own.

FRIENDS HELPING FRIENDS COLLAGE
(INDIVIDUAL AND GROUP)

Materials: various shapes of paper, paints, markers, poster board, glue or glue sticks

- Brainstorm together about ways friends help friends, encouraging the children to share ways they have been helped by others or have helped a friend.
- Have each child paint or draw a picture depicting someone helping another person.
- Glue the pictures to the poster board to make a collage of the children's artwork.

Additional idea: Take pictures of the children role-playing ways to help a friend. Make enough copies for all the children in the group to make their own collage to take home with them.

Display the collage during the closing celebration.

Kids Move

MOVE THE FRIEND
(GROUP)
Materials: beach towels or large bath towels, stuffed animals, boxes, small chairs, masking tape

- In preparation, mark a starting line and a finish line with tape. Set up obstacles, such as stacks of boxes or small chairs, between the lines.
- Divide the children into two or three groups, depending on the number of children. Give each group a towel and stuffed animal.
- Have a child hold each corner of the towel. Place a stuffed animal on it.
- Tell the children that they must get their friend to Jesus, but the way has some obstacles. They will want to get their friend to Jesus without dropping the friend along the way, so they will need to work together to get there.
- Repeat as often as needed so that everyone has a turn.
- Add more obstacles each time to make it trickier.

Closing
. . . .
For closing ideas, see page 7.

WORK WITH A FRIEND RACE
(PAIRS AND GROUP)
Materials: scarves, rope or tape

- In preparation, mark two places, a starting point and a turning-around point, with a short distance between for the race. Pair children by similar height.
- Tie the inside legs of the children together using a scarf, rope, or tape.
- Line the pairs up behind the starting line. They will need to go with their partner to the turning-around point and return to the starting line.
- Remind children that it is important to work together.

HELP CARRY THE LOAD
(GROUP)
Materials: Eight to 10 various-sized bags with handles, filled with various items to give bulk and weight; tape

- In preparation, mark start and finish lines with tape.
- Have the children line up at one end and place the bags at the other end.
- Have one child go to the other end, load up his or her arms with all the bags, carry them back to the starting line, and set them down.
- The next child loads up his or her arms with the bags and walks from the start to the finish and back again. Repeat until each child has had a turn.
- Talk as a group about how that worked.
- Do it again, but this time have the children work in pairs or small groups to complete the same task.
- Talk as a group about how that worked.
- The final time, let everyone work together to move the bags.
- Talk about the merits of working together as friends to make the task easier.

Session 5
Plant Seeds

The concepts in today's story focus more on the individual children and the way they each take the word of God into their lives. For most children this happens at a sub-conscious level. Notice that in the story Jesus describes a sower who was sowing his seeds freely and generously. Some of the seeds fell on unhelpful soil, while other seeds fell on good soil. Soil can change over the years and so can our hearts. Encourage the children to be reflective on the soil of their hearts. This lesson provides the opportunity for the children to stop and reflect.

The memory verse is Luke 8:11b: The seed is the word of God.

BIBLE TEXT
Luke 8:4-15
(additional texts: Matthew 13:1-23, Mark 4:1-20)

FAITH CHALLENGE
Seeds grow in good soil.

ADVANCE PREPARATION
- Read through the entire session and decide what you will do.
- Set up the space for the various activities.
- Practice the theme song or other music you may wish to sing.
- Gather supplies for the activities you choose to do.
- Prepare a snack (p. 12).
- Collect four transparent containers, each filled with a different type of soil (hard, rocky, thorny or weedy, good); seeds; and water. Rocky and weedy containers should have soil at the bottom but be mostly filled with the debris.

Kids Cluster

1. **Plan an activity for early arrivals.** Check page 6 for ideas.
2. **Welcome the children and gather for a time of singing** (p. 8). Be sure to include action songs, familiar songs, favorite songs, and new songs.
3. **Display the four soil containers.** Give seeds to four children and have each child put his or her seeds in one of the containers, pushing hard to get the seeds into the soil. Look at the containers and discuss with the children if the seeds will get to the soil. Water each container to show how the seeds might move or be soaked, and make note of where the water goes. Look at the container with good soil and note the difference in soil, seed placement, and water movement.
4. **Add that just like seeds need good soil,** so do the seeds (words) of Jesus need good soil to grow in our hearts. Remind the children that they need to tend their hearts and keep out the rocks and weeds so that the soil of their heart will remain open to the seeds (words) of Jesus.

Kids Know the Way . . .

1. **Begin by singing the theme song,** "Come and See" (p. 9).

2. **Introduce the theme of the day:** Seeds grow in good soil.

3. **Open your Bible to Luke 8:4-15.** Tell the children that the story tells us about a way to follow Jesus and that Jesus told a parable about soil and seeds. Remind the children that a parable is a story that uses common examples to explain difficult topics. In the story today, we find that our lives can be like the different types of soil we saw a few minutes ago. Jesus tells us in the parable that different people receive the seeds (words) of Jesus in different ways. Listen to the story to hear which kind of soil Jesus is looking for when he sows the seeds of his kingdom in our lives. Read or retell the story.

4. **Talk with the children about the different parts of the story.** Ask them:
   - How did the different people in the story respond to the word of God?
   - How are the different types of soil like different people?
   - How can we be like good soil when we hear God's word?

5. **This lesson asks us to think about our own lives** and the soil we carry within. You may want to lead a reflective prayer time. Keep it simple. Have the children spread out but remain within the sound of your voice. They may get comfortable and close their eyes. Lead them through a simple reflection time, inviting them to share their thoughts with Jesus. Say:

   Think about something great you did today. Tell Jesus. (*pause*)

   Think about something you did today that was not so great. Tell Jesus. (*pause*)

   Think of a time when you were hard to get along with. Tell Jesus. (*pause*)

   Think about a time today when you were at your best, when you shared a smile, were nice to someone, or gave a compliment. Tell Jesus. (*pause*)

   End with this prayer:
   Thank you, Jesus, for sowing your seeds in our lives. Sometimes those seeds fall on our good ground; sometimes they don't. Thank you for loving us no matter what. Amen.

Kids Create

PLANT A SEED IN GOOD GROUND
(INDIVIDUAL)

Materials: small flowerpots, markers or paints, soil, seeds or plants, water

- Give a flowerpot to each child and allow time to decorate it in a personal way.
- Review the different types of soil from the beginning of the session and explain the importance of good soil for plants.
- Help the children plant a seed in their soil and add a little water. Set the flowerpots in a sunny place.

Additional idea: Depending on the time of year, it may be best to plant a flower.

BIRD FEEDERS
(INDIVIDUAL)

Materials: pinecones, peanut butter or suet, birdseed, yarn, wax paper, plastic bags

- Help each child tie a piece of yarn around a pinecone to create a loop for hanging.
- Have the children use spoons to put peanut butter or suet on their pinecones.
- When the pinecones are coated, have the children roll them in birdseed until the peanut butter or suet is no longer showing.
- Place the pinecones on wax paper to dry.
- Put the pinecones in plastic bags for the children to take home. They can hang their pinecones outside as bird feeders.

TENDING THE SOIL OF YOUR HEART
(INDIVIDUAL)

Materials: 8.5 x 11 paper, colored pencils, markers or crayons

- Have the children fold their paper in half and then in half again to create four sections when unfolded.
- In each section of the paper, have the children complete one of the following sentences and draw an illustration to go along with it.

1. Something good that I can do is . . .
2. A talent I have is . . .
3. I know God is with me when . . .
4. I can talk to God when . . .

Kids Move

ACT IT OUT
(GROUP)

Read the text and have the children dramatize each scene with everyone playing the same role and changing roles throughout the story. Or, assign specific parts so that everyone has a different role. Encourage the children to think about staging elements, such as who stands where and what they do.

SOWER AND SEEDS COURSE
(PAIRS)

Materials: blindfolds, materials as described in the preparation

- In preparation, set up a large space with areas to represent the different types of soil from the biblical text. (examples: hard soil—cover the area in flat cardboard or plywood; rocky—cover the area with rocks; thorny/weedy—cover the area with twigs; good—cover the area with a green rug or a piece of green fabric)
- Divide the children into pairs and choose one child from each pair to be the "seed." Since seeds do not see where they are sown, blindfold the seed.
- Have the child who is not blindfolded give verbal directions to lead the seed to the good soil.

Closing
. . . .
For closing ideas, see page 7.

SAVE THE SEED
(GROUP)

Materials: green rug or piece of green cloth, one seed, paper cut into strips, pencils or pens

- Place the seed on the green cloth, which represents the good soil.
- Ask the children to talk about the thorns in life that might choke out the good growth, such as being unkind to one another, lying, talking bad about someone, etc. As each child offers an idea about what chokes out the good, write the idea on a strip of paper, ball it up, and lay it on or near the seed.
- Then, ask children to talk about things that keep soil in good shape, such as being friendly, giving a compliment, praying for someone, welcoming a new student at school, etc. As each child offers an idea about what keeps the soil in good shape, remove one of the papers from around the seed.
- Continue until the seed is once again free.

WEEDING PROJECT
(GROUP)

Depending on the time of year you are meeting, you might be able to arrange a service project to clear weeds. If there are flowerbeds that are in need of attention around the church or at someone's house, offer to help weed. Another possibility is to volunteer at a community garden.

Session 6
Share Gifts

6

Some of the children might be familiar with this story, as it is well used with children. Usually the version from John is used because of the reference to the small boy who shares his lunch so that all may be fed.

For this lesson the focus is on sharing, but the little boy does not appear in the Mark text. Instead of emphasizing the role of the child, this lesson focuses on what happens when people give from what they have to be used for the whole. This may be a large concept for children, but it is important in reinforcing that we are all a part of something larger. When we are able and willing to share our gifts, or in this case what we have, the whole community can benefit. Sharing our faith is one way to share the gifts we have received.

The memory verse is Mark 6:42: And all ate and were filled.

BIBLE TEXT
Mark 6:30-44

FAITH CHALLENGE
Jesus will use our gifts.

ADVANCE PREPARATION
- Read through the entire session, and decide what you will do.
- Set up the space for the various activities.
- Practice the theme song or other music you may wish to sing.
- Gather supplies for the activities you choose to do.
- Prepare a snack (p. 12).
- Gather crayons and small sheets of paper.

Kids Cluster

1. **Plan an activity for early arrivals.** Check page 6 for ideas.
2. **Welcome the children and gather for a time of singing** (p. 8). Be sure to include action songs, familiar songs, favorite songs, and new songs.
3. **Talk with the children about what it is like to work together.** Ask them:
   - Do you like working with others?
   - Is it easy to share supplies with each other?
   - What makes working with others a good experience?

   Explain that sometimes it is hard to work together and share supplies. But when we share what God has given us, we add more to life around us.
4. **Give each child several crayons.** Invite the children to draw a rainbow on their paper using red, orange, yellow, green, blue, indigo, and violet. If the children respond that they do not have enough crayons, encourage them to make a rainbow anyway. Remind the children to use their gifts (crayons), and to share their gifts with others. When we work together using our gifts, we can do some really great things.

45

Kids Know the Way...

1. **Begin by singing the theme song,** "Come and See" (p. 9).

2. **Introduce the theme of the day:** Jesus will use our gifts.

3. **Open your Bible to Mark 6:30-44.** Tell the children that people came from all over to hear Jesus preach and teach. In the story we will hear today, Jesus has been sharing his gift of preaching and teaching with many people. He wanted to get a little time away with his disciples, but as they were walking people recognized Jesus and followed him. In the story we will hear how the disciples gathered a gift from within the crowd that turned out to be a benefit to the whole crowd. Read or retell Mark 6:30-44.

4. **Talk with the children about the different parts of the story.** Ask them:

   • How much food do you think it would take to feed 5,000 people?
   • How did Jesus share his gifts with the crowd?
   • How did his disciples help him?
   • How did Jesus and the disciples show they cared about the people?
   • What did Jesus do with the gifts of food?

46

Kids Create

BLESSING BAGS
(INDIVIDUAL)

Materials: paper lunch bags, markers, stickers, small treats (such as fresh fruit or candy), unruled index cards

- Give the children lunch bags and invite them to decorate their bags.
- Have them write words of encouragement (for example, God loves you; I am thankful for you; Rejoice in the Lord) on the index cards.
- Put a few treats, such as fresh fruit or candy, into the bag.
- Arrange to take the bags to a local care center to share with residents.

SHARING MY GIFTS COUPONS
(INDIVIDUAL)

Materials: small pieces of paper, crayons, markers, colored pencils

- Talk about gifts we can share with others. They can be complex or simple. Examples include smiling, reading a book aloud, cleaning one's room, playing a song, singing a song, coloring a picture, laughing out loud, and offering a hug when someone feels sad.
- Have the children think of three or more gifts they can share with a friend, parent, brother, sister, or other family member.
- Demonstrate how to make coupons to give away as a way to share, but also to remind children that they have gifts to share!

Note: One wording suggestion for the coupon: I, (name), will share with you, (name), a gift of _____. You may redeem this coupon any Saturday of the month.

> I, (name), will share with you, (name), a gift of _____. You may redeem this coupon any Saturday of the month.

BRACELETS TO SHARE
(INDIVIDUAL)

Materials: leather or plastic lacing cut to size; green, red, yellow, blue, and pink beads

Children will make two bracelets, one to keep and one to give to a friend.

- Give each child two pieces of lacing and 10 beads, two of each color. Tie a knot about 4 in. / 10.2 cm from one end of each lacing.
- Children will string five beads onto each lacing. Tie knots at the opposite ends to secure the beads.
- Children may help each other tie the bracelets on their arms. The second bracelet should be given to a friend who is not at Kids Club.

Additional idea: Give each child a card with the information listed below to give along with the bracelet to encourage them to share about what they are learning at *Kids Can Know the Way*.

Kids Can Know the Way
Green—Jesus came to show us the way.
Red—We can follow the call of Jesus.
Yellow—We like to help our friends.
Blue—Jesus' word can grow in our hearts.
Pink—We share gifts with others.
Thanks for being my friend!

Kids Move

MIXED-UP PICNIC
(GROUP)
Materials: lunch bags; items for a simple picnic, such as cheese, crackers, grapes, napkins, cups, and drinks

- In preparation, put all of one item into one bag. All of the napkins go in one bag; all of the crackers go in another bag; etc.
- Give each child a bag to carry to a picnic area. When you arrive, have the children open their bags and tell them that they should begin eating. Soon they will realize they each have just one of the picnic items.
- Talk together about ways they can share so that everyone has some of everything.

WORK TOGETHER
(GROUP)
Materials: lunch bags, several simple puzzles

- In preparation, put each puzzle piece in a separate bag.
- Divide the children into groups who have pieces of the same puzzle.
- Have each child take one bag and gather with other children in their group. They should look inside the bag but not remove the contents.
- Ask the children to think to themselves about what they might do with the contents of their bag.
- Ask one child to take out his or her item. Ask more to do the same.
- Have the children ask each other what they should do. They will realize that they need each other to complete the puzzle.

MULTIPLYING LOAVES
(GROUP)
- Set boundaries for the game.
- Name one child as the "first loaf." The first loaf will tag other loaves (children) and then they will join hands.
- Each time a new loaf is added, he or she is the loaf that multiplies by tagging the next loaf. The last two added are the fish, and they get to start the next round.

Closing
For closing ideas, see page 7.

Session 7
Know the Shepherd

7

We may all have a person we can identify by simply hearing his or her voice. It could also be that someone has a name for us that only that person gets to use. We pray that each of the children who gather together knows what it is like to be known and for someone to think he or she is special.

Today's lesson is about Jesus knowing his sheep and finding them when they are lost. This story may be a curiosity for those who have not grown up around a farm or animals. This picture of Jesus as one who seeks us is a wonderful image to instill in children as way for them to know they are not alone.

The memory verse is Luke 15:6b: Rejoice with me, for I have found my sheep that was lost.

BIBLE TEXT
Luke 15:3-7 and Matthew 18:12-14

FAITH CHALLENGE
Jesus is the Good Shepherd.

ADVANCE PREPARATION
- Read through the entire session and decide what you will do.
- Set up the space for the various activities.
- Practice the theme song or other music you may wish to sing.
- Gather supplies for the activities you choose to do.
- Prepare a snack (p. 12).
- Hide small objects for each child around the room.
- Work with four children to practice reading the Psalm 23 choral reading on page 53.

Kids Cluster

1. **Plan an activity for early arrivals.** Check page 6 for ideas.
2. **Welcome the children and gather for a time of singing** (p. 8). Be sure to include action songs, familiar songs, favorite songs, and new songs.
3. **Tell the children that there are (objects) hidden around the room** for everyone. Give time for the children to search for their objects and then gather again as a group.
4. **Ask questions about searching, such as:**
   - Have you ever lost something that was very important to you?
   - How did you feel when you looked for it?
   - Has anyone ever been lost? How did you feel when you were found?
   Tell the children that today we will hear a story about how Jesus will always look for us if we get separated from him.

Kids Know the Way...

1. **Begin by singing the theme song,** "Come and See" (p. 9).

2. **Introduce the theme of the day:** Jesus is the Good Shepherd.

3. **Open your Bible to Luke 15:3-7 and Matthew 18:12-14.** Tell the children that in the hills around the area where Jesus lived there were lots of shepherds. These shepherds would tend their sheep in the hills around the city. It was very easy for a sheep to get separated from the rest of the flock, as there were lots of interesting places to explore in the hills. The story that we will hear is one that Jesus told to show how important each person is to him. Telling a story about sheep made sense to the people who were listening to him that day. Jesus wanted the people to know how much they meant to him. Read or retell the story from both Luke and Matthew.

4. **Talk with the children about the different parts of the story.** Ask them:
   - How do you think the sheep felt when it realized it was separated from the group?
   - How do you think the sheep felt when it was found?
   - Why did the shepherd search for the sheep until it was found?
   - What do you care about so much that you would search for it for a long time if it got lost?

5. **Have four children read the Psalm 23 choral reading on page 53.**

50

Kids Create

DECODE A VERSE
(INDIVIDUAL)

Materials: copies of the handout from page 55

- Distribute the handout to the children and go over the instructions for decoding the message.
- After all the children are finished, have them say the answer and repeat it several times. If needed, pair the younger and older students on this project.

Answer: And when he comes home, he calls together his friends and neighbors, saying to them, "Rejoice with me, for I have found my sheep that was lost."

REJOICE MURAL
(INDIVIDUAL OR GROUP)

Materials: mural paper, glue, scissors, crayons or markers, old magazines

Tell the children: Jesus was happy when he found the lost sheep. He rejoiced! What are things that make you happy and rejoice?

- Create a large mural. Invite the children to either draw or cut out pictures of things that make them happy and attach them to the mural paper.
- Help them to think beyond material possessions and instead focus on elements of the natural world, such as the sunrise, or on ways people help each other.
- Write "We rejoice!" at the bottom of the mural and hang it up for everyone to see. The mural can be pointed out during the closing celebration.

PAINT A PATH
(INDIVIDUAL)

Materials: paper, paints, pictures of different landscapes

Give the children some background information about shepherds in Jesus' time. Some shepherds lived and roamed the land with their sheep, searching for grass for the sheep to eat and water for them to drink. Other shepherds had their sheep in pens outside the village and would let their sheep outside the pens each day to roam the hills for grass and water. All of the shepherds called their sheep together every night. When they had their sheep gathered, they would count them to make sure all had arrived. If one was not there, they would go and search for it.

- Invite the children to paint a landscape and the path the shepherd would take to find the lost sheep.

Kids Move

FIND THE SHEEP
(GROUP)
Materials: enough small sheep shapes for each child to find one (p. 54)

- In preparation, hide the sheep outside or inside your building, as would be done for an Easter egg hunt.
- Send the children to find the lost sheep.
- After they find one sheep, encourage them to help their friends.

SHEEP IN A HAYSTACK
(INDIVIDUAL)
Materials: one small stuffed sheep, storage container filled with polyester batting or cotton balls, blindfold (optional). You may use several stuffed sheep and several containers.

- In preparation, hide the sheep inside the container among the filler.
- Have the children find the sheep without looking into the container, or while blindfolded.

Closing
For closing ideas, see page 7.

HEAR THE SHEPHERD'S VOICE
(GROUP)
Materials: props to make a sheep pen; a noisemaker such as a bell, recorder, harmonica, small drum, or tambourine

- Have everyone use the supplies to make a sheep pen large enough that all the children can stand inside.
- Designate a shepherd and give him or her the noisemaker.
- After a pause, the shepherd will walk around and sound the noisemaker. The shepherd should move about the whole area.
- When the sheep (children) hear the shepherd calling with the noisemaker, they should return to the sheep pen.
- After the sheep are gathered, the shepherd will count to see that all have returned. If not, go find the lost sheep!

LISTEN TO ONE ANOTHER
(GROUP)

- Have the children sit in a circle. Explain that they will practice listening with their ears and looking with their eyes, just as the shepherd had to do when searching for the lost sheep.
- Have one child at a time say how he or she is feeling: I am happy; I am sad; I am mad; I am bored; etc. At the same time, have the child use body language or tone of voice to either agree or disagree with the statement. You may need to demonstrate.
- The rest of the children must decide how the person is really feeling.

PSALM 23
CHORAL READING
Have four children read. Invite those not reading to close their eyes and picture the different scenes in their mind.

1: The Lord is my shepherd,

2: **I shall not want.**

3: *He makes me lie down in green pastures;*

4: ***he leads me beside still waters;***

1: he restores my soul.

2: **He leads me in right paths for his name's sake.**

3: *Even though I walk through the darkest valley,*

4: ***I fear no evil;***

1: for you are with me;

2: **your rod and your staff**

3: *they comfort me.*

4: ***You prepare a table before me***

1: in the presence of my enemies;

2: **you anoint my head with oil;**

3: *my cup overflows.*

4: ***Surely goodness and mercy***

1: shall follow me

2: **all the days of my life,**

3: *and I shall dwell*

4: ***in the house of the Lord***

All: my whole life long.

A	B	C	D	E	F	G	H	I	J	K	L	M
♋	♌	♍	♎	♏	♐	♑	♒	♓	er	&	●	○

N	O	P	Q	R	S	T	U	V	W	X	Y	Z
■	□	⚑	✈	☼	♦	❄	◆	❖	⊕	✠	☐	⌘

And when he comes home, he calls together his

friends and neighbors, saying to them, "Rejoice

with me, for I have found my sheep that was lost."

Session 8
Share the Way

The story of Mary and Martha is often used to instruct us on choosing a better way and setting priorities. We learn in the book of John that Martha declares that she knows that Jesus is the Messiah—in fact, she is the first person to do so. Martha approaches hosting in her home a bit differently than her sister, but that does not make her any less hospitable.

The focus of this lesson is on slowing down so that we do not miss out on the good stuff that is happening. By showing a warm welcome to everyone we meet, we can share Jesus. Jesus told Martha that she should spend a little more time paying attention to what was going on around her so that she would not miss out on anything, especially on what Jesus was teaching.

The memory verse is Luke 10:38b: Martha welcomed him into her home.

BIBLE TEXT
Luke 10:38-42

FAITH CHALLENGE
We can welcome others.

ADVANCE PREPARATION
- Read through the entire session and decide what you will do.
- Set up the space for the various activities.
- Practice the theme song or other music you may wish to sing.
- Gather supplies for the activities you choose to do.
- Prepare a snack (p. 12).

Kids Cluster

1. **Plan an activity for early arrivals.** Check page 6 for ideas.
2. **Welcome the children and gather for a time of singing** (p. 8). Be sure to include action songs, familiar songs, favorite songs, and new songs.
3. **Ask the children many questions at a fast pace,** not allowing time for responses. (Examples: What color is your hair? How was your day? Did you have fun today? What did you eat for lunch? How did you get here? Were you mad at anyone today? Were you kind to your friends? Are you tired? Did you sleep well last night?) Continue the questions and see if anyone expresses frustration or asks you to slow down and wait for an answer.

   Ask the children how they felt about all of the questions. Allow time for responses. Share about a time when you were so busy that you did not wait or did not pay attention to another person. Assure the children that we might all have times like that, but that even if we are busy it is good to slow down so we do not miss out on the good stuff.

Kids Know the Way...

1. **Begin by singing the theme song,** "Come and See" (p. 9).
2. **Introduce the theme of the day:** We can welcome others.
3. **Open the Bible to Luke 10:38-42.** Tell the children that there are lots of stories in the Bible about Jesus eating in the homes of friends and in the homes of people he had just met. Jesus was quick to go into people's homes and share a meal with them. When we have someone coming to our house, maybe our parents ask us to do some extra chores, put our things away, or even give up our bed for the guests. Sometimes it is extra work to have people over to our house, but Jesus reminds us to be hospitable, kind, and welcoming to whomever we meet. Today we will hear about two sisters who did things differently when Jesus came to their house. Let's see how they each prepared for guests. Read or retell the story.
4. **Talk with the children about the different parts of the story.** Ask them:
   - What do you think about Martha getting ready for guests?
   - Was it important that food was prepared?
   - Who else would have done it if Martha had not?
   - Is it important to have the house and food ready for guests?
   - Should Mary have helped Martha?
   - What do you think Mary wanted to learn from Jesus?
   - Why do you think the sisters chose to do different things?

Kids Create

WAYS TO WELCOME
(SMALL GROUPS)
Materials: paper, pencils
- Divide the children into groups of two or three.
- Give each group a piece of paper and have them brainstorm ways they can make someone feel welcome. They should choose one way and create a skit to act it out.
- Have the groups share their skits with each other.

STORY STRIP
(INDIVIDUAL, PAIRS)
Materials: long strips of paper, three or four boxes, colored pencils
- Give each child a strip of paper and colored pencils. Have the children think through a time they were welcoming to another person.
- Give them some ideas about how to break their story into three or four different scenes.
- Let them turn their experience into a story strip.
- When all the children are done, have them share their story with a partner.

PLAN A PARTY
(GROUP)
Materials: cards for invitations; pencils, markers, crayons, or colored pencils
- Help the children plan a party for the closing celebration. Have them think about what they learned over these last eight sessions that would be important to share with others. Ask them how those things could be shared during the closing celebration.
- Decide on a refreshment menu that the children can prepare and serve.
- Have the children create invitations to give to family and friends.

Be sure to talk about ways to make others feel welcome during the closing celebration.

Kids Move

MAKE A VISIT
(GROUP)

If there are people in the neighborhood who are homebound, or if there is a care center nearby, arrange to take the children for a visit. Make simple preparations for the visit, perhaps having children draw pictures to give to the residents, or plan a few songs to sing or Bible stories to dramatize. Encourage the children to enjoy the responses of the people they are visiting.

ROLE PLAY
(GROUP)
Materials: props and costumes

Review before starting: It is easy to be nice to our friends, but what about others? God wants us to be nice to our friends, but God also wants us to be nice to people we don't know as well. What would you do in the following situations?

- Divide the class into groups of two or three, according to the parts needed to plan and act out the following situations. Provide a box of appropriate props and costumes.

Situation 1: You are playing with your best friend, Jose, at his house. He gets mad at you and tells you to go home. Later that day, he calls on the phone to see if you want to play.

Situation 2: You are at your good friend Latisha's house playing. She brings out her toys but won't let you play with her favorite doll. The next day she comes to your house and wants to play with your favorite doll.

Situation 3: Sergi had a birthday party and invited everyone in your class except you. Two weeks later it is your birthday and you were planning to invite everyone in your class. Will you invite Sergi?

HOSPITALITY CAFÉ
(GROUP)
Materials: table and chairs for half of the group, simple snack items in separate bowls, plates, cups, napkins, tablecloths for each table

- Set up a simple café for the children to serve each other. While half of the group reads and relaxes, the other half gets the café ready by setting the table with plates, cups, and napkins.
- When they are ready, have the children invite the other group to come to the Hospitality Café. Children should pull out chairs for their guests and serve them food and water. Remind the servers to make sure that the water glasses stay full and that those seated have what they need.
- When the guests are finished, have the servers clear the tables while the guests return to reading and relaxing.
- When all is cleaned up, have the groups switch roles and repeat the process.
- When both groups are finished, ask how it felt to be part of the different groups.

ROOM FOR MORE
(GROUP)
Materials: CD player, lively music, three to five Hula-Hoops or mats

- In preparation, place three to five Hula-Hoops or mats on the floor.
- Play music and invite the children to move in time to it, avoiding the hoops or mats.
- When the music stops, all must step into a hoop or onto a mat.
- Repeat, removing a hoop. The children will have to fit into fewer hoops.
- Play until all the children are squeezed into one hoop.
- Talk about the invitation from Jesus to make room for everyone.

Closing
For closing ideas, see page 7.

Closing Celebration
Friends Share the Way

(clos-ing)

Kids can know the way, and in this lesson kids can share the way. Today's session focuses on the children sharing what they have learned in the previous nine lessons with others in their lives. This is also a chance for the children and adults to work together on some activities that show the way their life stories interweave, just like they do with Jesus.

BIBLE TEXT
Luke 8:1-3

FAITH CHALLENGE
Jesus' friends share the way.

ADVANCE PREPARATION
- Read through the entire session and decide what you will do.
- Set up the space for the various activities.
- Practice the theme song or other music you may wish to sing.
- Gather supplies for the activities you choose to do.
- Prepare a snack (p. 12).

Kids Cluster

1. **Plan an activity for early arrivals.** Check page 6 for ideas.
2. **Welcome the children and their guests.** Gather for a time of singing. Be sure to include action songs, familiar songs, favorite songs, and new songs. If there are songs that children especially enjoyed during Kids Club, be sure to include them.
3. **Encourage the children to share a good memory** or one of their favorite Kids Club activities with their guests. Next, ask the children to share one thing they learned from Kids Club. If memory verses were learned, present them to the group.

Kids Know the Way ...

1. **Begin by singing the theme song,** "Come and See" (p. 9).

2. **Introduce the theme of the day:** Jesus' friends share the way.

3. **Open the Bible to Luke 8:1-3.** Explain that over the last few weeks together, we learned a lot about Jesus. Review the stories by offering a reminder of a story and having children add details about their time together. Add that this last Bible story tells us what Jesus and his followers did. Jesus was not alone as he shared—his disciples and friends told people about Jesus too. As friends of Jesus, we are the ones who get to share the stories of Jesus with the people we meet. Read or retell the story.

4. **Talk with the children about the different parts of the story.** Ask them:
   - Where did Jesus go?
   - What did he tell the people he met?
   - Who went with him?
   - Who are some of your friends who also know the story of Jesus?
   - What should we do now that we know these stories?

Response Activities

Use Kids Can Create or Kids Can Move activities that were not used during previous sessions.

KNOW THE WAY MURAL

Materials: additional supplies for the guests

- Have the children show their guests the journey mural. Invite the guests to add their own life stories to the mural.

SHARE THE STORY

Materials: paper, small footprint cutouts (p. 65), markers or crayons, printed Scripture verses from each lesson

- In preparation, set up a table with the Scriptures from each lesson, sheets of paper, and crayons and markers.
- Include the following written instructions:
  1. Choose some footprint cutouts.
  2. Choose a few of the Scripture texts to read together.
  3. Pick one thing from the story that you want to share with others and write it on the footprint.
  4. After you have done this for several of the stories, glue the footprints onto the paper in the form of a path to remind you to share the way with others.

ACT OUT THE BIBLE STORIES

Materials: costumes and props as needed

- Several of the Bible stories in this series lend themselves to dramatization. Have a few small groups of children and adults select a Bible story and then work together to act it out.
- Make the event more fun by having the children be the directors and the adults be actors!

DON'T HIT THE TRAIL HUNGRY

Materials: peanuts, M&M's, pretzels, raisins or other dried fruit, small bags, stickers

- In preparation, set up a snack station.
- Have people make their own little snack bag to take with them. Encourage them to make a snack bag they can share with someone else.
- Have them write one of the memory verses on a sticker and stick it to the bag.

HAVE YOU SEEN JESUS?

Materials: a small figure that represents Jesus

- Designate someone to be one of Jesus' parents.
- Give the small figure to one person without the others seeing.
- Divide the children and adults in groups of four to six.
- Have the parent move to different groups, asking specific people if they have seen Jesus.
- If the answer is no, the parent must move out of the group.
- Repeat in the different circles until Jesus is found.

PRAYER POCKETS

Materials: card stock, crayons, markers, unruled index cards, stapler or tape, magnets with sticky backs

- Give each person a piece of card stock to decorate.
- Have people fold the card stock in half and secure the short sides with staples or tape.
- Invite them to write the names of people they would like pray for each day on index cards.
- Place the cards inside the pocket.
- Attach a magnet on the back to secure to the refrigerator.

PASS THE MESSAGE

Materials: Hula-Hoop

- Have everyone stand in a circle. Have one person put the Hula-Hoop on one arm and then have everyone join hands.
- Direct the group to pass the Hula-Hoop all the way around the circle without letting go of each other's hands.

This is a great way to get the adults and children to work together.

Closing

For closing ideas, see page 7.

64

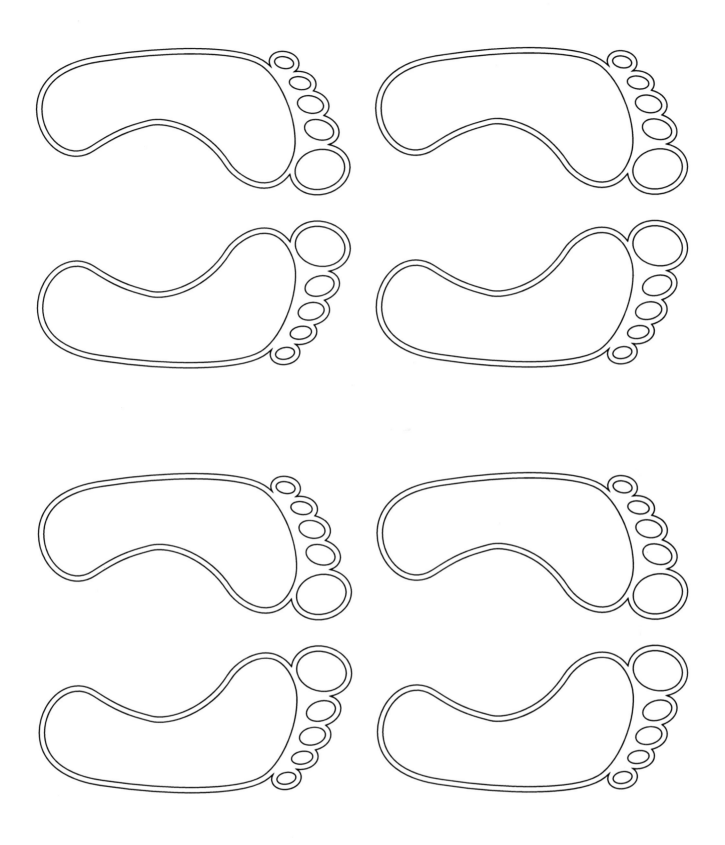

Evaluation
Tell us what you think

· ·

Congregation _____

Your Name (optional) _____

Address _____

City _____ **Province/State** _____ **Code**_____

1. I have these comments about _Kids Can Know the Way_ regarding session compo-
    nents (faith challenge, kids create, kids move, etc.).

    _____
    _____
    _____
    _____
    _____
    _____
    _____
    _____

2. I have these comments about how the program worked for us (time frame, ses-
    sion flow, user-friendliness, etc.).

    _____
    _____
    _____
    _____
    _____
    _____
    _____

Additional comments:

_____
_____
_____
_____
_____
_____

To return
· · · · · · · · · · · · · ·
Please make copies of
this form or use the
online form at www
.MennoMedia.org/
kidscanclub.

Complete form and
send to:
Kids Can Know the Way
MennoMedia
1251 Virginia Ave.
Harrisonburg, VA 22802

Also check out:

KIDS CAN BE BLESSED

Kids Can Be Blessed invites kids to learn how to put the Beatitudes into practice. Using Jesus' words as the example, kids will better understand how they can live the Beatitudes and be blessed as they make decisions, interact with others, and seek God's ways in their daily lives.

KIDS CAN CATCH THE LOVE

Kids Can Catch the Love helps kids explore God's love. Stories from the Old Testament illustrate God's love for humanity as well as ways in which people show their love for God. Even when it is difficult, the characters remain faithful to the God they love because they know that God loves them. Just as God loved and cared for those in the stories, God loves and cares for us.

KIDS CAN LIVE UPSIDE DOWN

Through *Kids Can Live Upside-Down*, kids will learn that when they live upside down, the world will look different! In God's kingdom, Jesus calls us to serve others, accept God's forgiveness, worship God sincerely, and love our enemies.

KIDS CAN MAKE PEACE

Using Jesus as an example, *Kids Can Make Peace* teaches kids how they can become peacemakers in a complex world, how they can cherish and protect the earth's natural resources, resolve conflicts, and cultivate a sense of inner peace.

KIDS CAN GET IT RIGHT

Kids Can Get It Right uses Old Testament stories to illustrate how to live in right relationships with each other and with God. Kids will explore how values build character and be inspired by the faithfulness of God's people.

KIDS CAN CLUB

Ten-session all-in-one resources for children's clubs, midweek, Sunday night, camp, or other settings.

www.MennoMedia.org/kidscanclub

MennoMedia
An agency of Mennonite Church USA and Mennonite Church Canada

CPSIA information can be obtained at www.ICGtesting.com
Printed in the USA
BVOW050606040413

317239BV00006B/73/P

9 780836 196962